A Walking Tour
of Dublin Churches

illustrated by Liam C. Martin

VERITAS

First published 1988 by
Veritas Publications
7-8 Lower Abbey Street
Dublin 1

Copyright © Veritas Publications 1988

Illustrations copyright © Liam C. Martin

ISBN 1 85390 045 1

*The publishers are grateful to the following for their
assistance in the compilation of this volume:*
Rev. Kenneth Wright, Dean T.N.D.C. Salmon, Fr Des
O'Byrne, Fr Marcellus Murphy, Rev. Mother
Concepta, Fr Philip Kelly, Fr Des Dockery, Fr Brian
O'Sullivan, Dean Victor Griffin, Fr John Byrne, Fr
Anthony Gaughan, Fr John Fitzpatrick, Fr Aidan
Burke, Rev. David Weakliam, Anne O'Connor.

Typesetting by Printset & Design Ltd, Dublin
Printed in the Republic of Ireland by
Criterion Press Ltd, Dublin

CONTENTS

This volume is dedicated
to all who work for peace in the world.

FOREWORD

Much of the history of early Ireland is written into the great monastic ruins at Glendalough, Clonmacnoise, Monasterboice and sacred artefacts like the Cross of Cong and the Ardagh Chalice. In like manner the relevance of religious belief to the history of Dublin is immense and lasting. Many of the present street names, Mary Street, Abbey Street, Thomas Street, Bride Street, come from great monasteries on whose lands present day Dublin was built. The very city of Dublin began with the building of a stockade around ships to protect them from marauding Vikings whose primary purpose was to plunder the wealth of the Irish monasteries.

In the old Irish settlement of Dublin were four churches of Celtic foundation, St Bride, St Michael-le-Pole, St Kevin and St Patrick. However, among the many spires and towers of the medieval parish churches, two dominated the skyline: the present day Church of Ireland cathedrals of Christ Church and St Patrick. Christ Church, the earlier, was within the original walls of the old city. St Patrick's was built by Archbishop John Comyn and dedicated on St Patrick's Day 1192. The unroofed portion of St Audoen's Church represents a Norman foundation of circa 1200.

A Walking Tour of Dublin Churches is a journey back into the faith story of the Dublin people. If the church buildings which still remain from early Dublin could speak, they would tell stories of fidelity, pain, poverty, joy and expectation.

Following the Danish invasion many more churches were established. The desire to worship God has never been far from the hearts of the people of Dublin. In this book you will find 'churches old and new'. Some were built down back lanes during the Penal days. Others, of new and exciting design, testify to the faith of today's citizens.

A church building is an expression of faith. In it worship was to be offered in the beauty of holiness. It is the expression in stone of a way of life based on belief in God as revealed in Christ Jesus. Cathedrals and churches fit into the mainstream of the life of the community. They

5

are a constant reminder 'that we are continuous with a reality which is akin'. They speak of beauty and eternal life. The atmosphere is one of hallowed silence and timelessness. Here men and women may see a vision of unity of peace. Though still and silent in stone, a church, by its very existence, points to a life beyond life.

The churches whose stories are told and whose facades are represented by Liam C. Martin in these pages are part of the heritage of the city of Dublin and in a special way belong to all the citizens. Their doors stand open to all who spend some time in prayer in each. In prayer we join in spirit with the present citizens of Dublin and with their ancestors of ages past.

T.N.D.C. Salmon
Dean of Christ Church

KEY TO MAP (pp. 36-37)

1. St Mary's Pro-Cathedral, Marlborough Street
2. The Rotunda Chapel, Parnell Square
3. Monastery and Church of St Alphonsus,
   St Alphonsus Road
4. St Columba's Church, Iona Road
5. St Joseph's Church, Berkeley Road
6. The Black Church, St Mary's Place
7. St Saviour's Church, Dominick Street
8. St Mary's Church, Capel Street
9. St Michan's Church, Church Street
10. The Church of Adam & Eve, Merchant's Quay
11. The Augustinian Church, Thomas Street
12. St Catherine's Church, Thomas Street
13. St Catherine's Church, Meath Street
14. The Church of St Nicholas of Myra, Francis Street
15. St Audoen's Church, Cornmarket
16. St Audoen's Church, High Street
17. Christ Church Cathedral, Christ Church Place
18. St Patrick's Cathedral, Patrick Street
19. St Werburgh's Church, Werburgh Street
20. Church of the Most Holy Trinity, Dublin Castle
21. Church of Our Lady of Mount Carmel,
    Whitefriars Street
22. St Teresa's Church, Clarendon Street
23. St Andrew's Church, St Andrew Street
24. The Blessed Sacrament Chapel, D'Olier Street
25. The Penal Day Chapel, Townsend Street
26. St Andrew's Church, Westland Row
27. St Stephen's Church, Mount Street Crescent
28. St Mary's Church, Haddington Road
29. Our Lady Seat of Wisdom (University Church),
    St Stephen's Green
30. The Unitarian Church, St Stephen's Green
31. Our Lady of Refuge, Rathmines Road

ST MARY'S PRO-CATHEDRAL, MARLBOROUGH STREET

Few buildings have such a close association with significant moments in the political and religious history of Ireland as St Mary's Pro-Cathedral has had for close on two centuries. Even its original proposed site had to be foregone for political reasons.

When Archbishop Troy wanted to replace the little penal-time 'mass-house' of St Mary's in Liffey Street with a dignified church in the city centre, he originally hoped that it could be built on a site which was made available by the widening of Sackville Street (later O'Connell Street) in 1796. However it was feared that such a bold step might only delay or jeopardise Catholic Emancipation, so Dr Troy's attention was directed to a nearby, less conspicuous spot, leaving the Sackville Street property to become the site of the new General Post Office.

The alternative site was Lord Annesley's town house, on the corner of Marlborough Street and Elephant Lane (later Cathedral Street). The site was purchased in trust in 1803, but it was twelve years later before sufficient funds could be collected to enable building to begin.

The design chosen was that attributed to John Sweetman of Raheny, who was a political exile in Paris following the 1798 rebellion, and his plan combines a variety of styles. The front portico is a copy of the Temple of Theseus in Athens, and the Doric columns rise without bases from the podium or floor of the church. Three statues adorn the top — Mary the Mother of God flanked by the two diocesan patrons, St Kevin and St Laurence O'Toole.

The interior is more Roman in style than Grecian and closely resembles the Church of Saint Philippe du Roule in Paris, a short distance from Sweetman's lodgings. However, a major alteration from Sweetman's design was the addition of a dome — 'a beautiful deformity' according to one objector.

After a protracted fund-raising struggle, the great opening day finally arrived, and on 14 November 1825 St Mary's was the scene of great rejoicing when Archbishop Daniel Murray performed the dedication ceremony. At the reception afterwards Daniel O'Connell concluded his speech with words as apt today as they were in 1825,

> 'If all classes of Irishmen were united, if the demon of discord was cast out from among them, what a happy country, how blessed beyond example Ireland should be.'

O'Connell died in Genoa in 1847. His remains were brought home by ship and, amid scenes of universal grief, borne from Custom House Quay to the Pro-Cathedral where the coffin lay for four days on a great catafalque. The whole church was draped in black.

The Pro-Cathedral has also been the scene of farewells to other great Irish statesmen, among them Arthur Griffith, Michael Collins, Eamon De Valera and, more recently, Sean MacBride.

Above all, this great church belongs to the people of Dublin, who know it affectionately as the 'Pro'. Every day there is a constant stream of people dropping in to light a candle and say a prayer. It is a living church. It continues to be as Archbishop Troy wanted it to be, a heart for the city and an active house of God.

Opening hours
7.45 am - 5.45 pm daily

THE ROTUNDA CHAPEL, PARNELL SQUARE

The foundation stone for the Rotunda Hospital was laid in 1757. It was designed by Richard Cassells who was famous for his designs of the Bank of Ireland, Tyrone House and Leinster House. Dr Mosse was principally responsible for the construction of the hospital as he spent virtually all his private means on the project and then set about obtaining a considerable amount of money from Parliament and the Dublin people towards its completion. He laid out the grounds as public gardens to be used by everyone.

The chapel itself is beautifully designed inside. The ceiling is unique and different from anything else in the city in that it is beautifully stuccoed. There is a console over the communion table which supports a lamb in *alto relievo*. Above this is a decorated canopy and on each side is a life-sized angel.

On the north side of the ceiling is a figure representing Faith while over the communion table is one portraying Charity and finally, on the south side, is a third, representing Hope. Moses holding the Ten Commandments can be seen above the organ with a corresponding figure of an angel blowing the trumpet. All these figures were designed by Cremeillon and were actually made by two Italian sculptors, the Francini Brothers.

Opening hours
Open all day

10

MONASTERY AND CHURCH OF ST ALPHONSUS, ST ALPHONSUS ROAD

The site of the present monastery and church of St Alphonsus was originally intended for the proposed Catholic University of Ireland. The foundation stone was blessed on 20 July 1862 in the presence of twenty-four archbishops and bishops. For various reasons that project had to be abandoned. In 1872 part of the land was acquired by the Redemptoristine Sisters. On 18 July the first stone of the new church and monastery was laid. It was the same stone which ten years before had been blessed for the Catholic University.

The dedication of the new church, which was designed by Ashlin, took place on 27 September 1875. The stone work depicting scenes from the life of Christ was executed by Italian workmen.

The magnificent marble high altar with its frontispiece of Leonardo da Vinci's Last Supper came from Rome. So also did the beautiful picture of Our Lady of Perpetual Help — the second to come to Ireland. The carved, wooden statues came from Munich. That of St Columba presented in 1882, was blessed by the chaplain, Fr Joseph Marmon, Holy Cross College, Clonliffe. He later became the renowned Abbot Columba Marmion OSB, Maredsous Abbey, Belgium.

Opening hours

Daily Mass   7.00 am Weekdays
Daily Benediction   9.00 am Saturday and Sunday
Visitors who wish to see the church at other times will be welcome.

ST COLUMBA'S CHURCH, IONA ROAD

St Columba's Church has a relatively short history but is interesting nonetheless. On 7 August 1903 the first stone was laid, just three days before Pius X was chosen as Pope. Therefore St Columba's was the first building in Christendom to have the new Pope's name engraved on its cornerstone.

By 1905 the church was ready to be opened and on 15 October it was blessed and dedicated to St Columba who is thought to have spent some time in the area during the sixth century. An interesting problem arose however in that there was no actual road leading to the church. The landlord would only grant building leases so St Columba's was faced with a difficult situation. The problem was solved eventually with the purchase of nine acres on condition that six houses, with the value of £500 each, would be built. The houses were completed, the road was opened and was then consecrated as Iona Road.

St Columba's, which was a subdivision of the original Berkeley Road church, cost £13,500 to build and was designed by Ashlin and Coleman. It was built on land which was at one time the property of the Redemptorist nuns.

The interior of the church is interesting because most of the architectural details are of Celtic design. Details to be noted include the beautiful marble high altar and the stained glass windows in the apse which depict the seven sacraments.

Opening hours
7.30 am - 8.30 pm daily

ST JOSEPH'S CHURCH, BERKELEY ROAD

This church began life as chapel of ease to St Michan's Roman Catholic Church, Halston Street. Prior to the 1860s the north-east side of Halston Street parish was rural, and stretched all the way to the village of Drumcondra. In 1870, James McMahon, parish priest of Halston Street, erected a wooden chapel to accommodate the families moving into Berkeley Road. On Sunday 6 September 1874, the foundation stone of the future church was laid by Cardinal Cullen. The official opening took place six years later, on Sunday 18 April 1880.

The new church, designed by O'Neill and Byrne, is in the neo-gothic style. The contractor was James Cormack of Talbot Street. The exterior is of granite, from the quarries at Ballyknockan, Co. Wicklow. A square belfry was added in its present position in 1890.

The interior includes beautiful arches of cream-coloured Caen stone, pillars of Midleton marble and a high vaulted ceiling of pitch pine and memel. The corbels were carefully sculpted and finished, the work of the firm of stonemasons, Pearse and Sharpe. The high altar is of Sicilian marble, relieved by pillars of rare yellow Mexican marble.

In 1890 St Joseph's became an independent parish. However, in 1902 the Archbishop constituted the new parish of St Columba, Iona Road. Eighty years later, in July 1983, Archbishop Dermot Ryan invited a community of Discalced Carmelites to assume care of the parent parish, St Joseph's itself.

Opening hours
7.30 am - 8.30 pm daily

ST MARY'S CHAPEL OF EASE — THE BLACK CHURCH, ST MARY'S PLACE

St Mary's Chapel of Ease, or the Black Church, was completed in 1830 and designed by the famous architect John Semple. The stone used in its construction was calpstone which gives it a black hue when wet, hence the name, the Black Church. The church was originally built as a chapel of ease to St Mary's on Mary Street.

The Black Church, from the outside, seems like an elegant example of attenuated Gothic. However, the interior is actually quite unusual which is not surprising as John Semple was known for his unique work. Maurice Craig in his book, *Dublin 1660-1860,* describes the interior very well. He says it has 'neither walls nor ceilings; instead it has an unbelievable parabolic vault which takes the place of both'.

The vault itself is built on the Mycenean Principle — it is laid in flat courses which oversail one another. In the west gallery there are enormous Scotch – baronial corbels, a timber and plaster structure imitating stone. St Mary's also has a very striking needle spire.

Various legends surround St Mary's Chapel of Ease, one of which Austin Clarke recalls in the title of his autobiography, *Twice around the Black Church.* This refers to a local superstition about meeting the devil if one walked around the church a certain number of times. The estimated number of circuits required in order to meet the devil varied from person to person.

The Black Church was closed and reopened a number of times. However, in 1962 it was finally secularised and bought by Dublin County Council. It is now used to house exhibitions.

Opening hours
Temporarily closed for repairs

ST SAVIOUR'S CHURCH, DOMINICK STREET

St Saviour's Church, Dominick Street, is one of the finest examples of the Gothic Revival in Ireland. The foundation stone was laid on 8 September 1852 by the Archbishop of Dublin, Dr Cullen, and the church was opened on 15 January 1861. The architect was J. J. McCarthy and the money to build it came, for the most part, from the pennies of the poor who then lived in the locality.

J. J. McCarthy, the architect, was probably the most notable of the pupils of Pugin, and St Saviour's Church evoked exactly the atmosphere of worship which the Gothic style sought to express. The church was reconstructed in the 1970s to adapt it to the liturgical reforms of the Second Vatican Council. The architects were Tyndal, Hogan and Hurley. Ray Carroll designed the tabernacle and pillar. The crucifix is by Benedict Tutty, OSB and the picture in the apse is by Patrick Pye. Especially worthy of note is Hogan's Pieta under the Holy Name Altar.

The church and priory replace an earlier Dominican church in Little Denmark Street. In the eighteenth century the Dominicans ministered in a modest penal day chapel in Bridge Street. The medieval foundation was on the site now occupied by the Four Courts.

Opening hours
Open all day

ST MARY'S ABBEY CHAPTER HOUSE, CAPEL STREET

This is almost the only surviving piece of the most important Cistercian Abbey in medieval Dublin. The door on its southern wall leads into a high narrow passage. The door seems modern but the passage is probably an ancient 'slype'. The 'slype', or covered passage, leads east to other parts of the Abbey.

About 1886, Sir Thomas Drew, the architect, embarked upon a clever plan to reconstruct the layout of St Mary's Abbey. He based his ideas on the fact that the Cistercians, because of their strict rules, used a standard plan for their abbeys. Therefore he guessed that the position of the high altar and the main body of the church must have been about fifty feet north of the Chapter House, which still existed. In 1886 some excavations were carried out which resulted in the recovery of some medieval tiles but the position of the Abbey still remained in doubt.

The Chapter House has great historical value. In 1534, Silken Thomas threw down the Sword of State before the councillors and renounced his allegiance to the English here. By 1700 most of the Abbey had disappeared. In fact its stones were used in 1678 to build Essex Bridge (Capel Street Bridge). Today the only surviving remnant of the Abbey is the statue of Our Lady of Dublin which is now enshrined in the Carmelite Church in Whitefriar Street.

ST MICHAN'S, CHURCH OF IRELAND

St Michan's occupies the site of an old Danish church of the eleventh century. Since approximately 1563 it has been Church of Ireland. At the beginning of this century the body of the church was taken down and the present building erected.

The adjoining cemetery was for many years a popular burial place. The remains of such people as the Sheares Brothers, Rev. W. Jackson and Oliver Bond may be found there.

St Michan's has a spacious interior with some interesting examples of old tombs. An effigy of the Danish bishop and confessor, St Michan, can be found at the south side of the chancel. The church plate includes an early seventeenth century copper gilt *repoussé* and also a silver gilt chalice, the stem and base of which date from 1516.

Opening hours

Mon-Fri	10.00 am - 12.45 pm
	2.00 pm - 4.45 pm
Sat	10.00 am - 12.45 pm

There is a charge of £1 for adults and 50p for children to see the vaults.

THE CHURCH OF ADAM AND EVE, MERCHANT'S QUAY

We in Ireland love to point out our Mass Rocks, those old stones in remote glens and on sheltered hillsides, where, in the dark days of persecution, our priests offered the Holy Sacrifice. Adam and Eve, in the very heart of Dublin, is just such a place. The Franciscans, right under the shadow of Dublin Castle, ministered to the spiritual needs of the people.

Expelled from their friary in Francis Street — where the Church of St Nicholas now stands — the friars finally settled in a small house in Cook Street at the back of a tavern called Adam and Eve. Each Sunday the people walked boldly to the inn, through the door of Adam and Eve and into the room where the friars offered Mass.

Then the priest-hunters came on the scene, and on St Stephen's Day, 1629, the Protestant Archbishop himself led a body of soldiers into Cook Street and the tavern. The two friars were taken prisoner — but as they were marching off in the midst of their captors, the women of the neighbourhood attacked the attackers, freed the friars, and put the Archbishop and his soldiers to flight.

Remaining around the vicinity, the friars still looked after the faithful people. In 1743, while Mass was being offered in Cook Street, the loft serving as a chapel collapsed and the celebrant and nine people were killed.

In 1834 the foundation stone of the new church was laid. The district is sacred ground; in no uncertain manner has the old saying been fulfilled, that the Church prospers on ground made holy by the blood of martyrs.

Opening hours
Weekdays   7.00 am - 9.00 pm
Closed Sunday afternoon

AUGUSTINIAN CHURCH, JOHN'S LANE

The Augustinians have been in Dublin since around 1280 and in the John's Lane area for the past 300 years. The present church was commenced in 1862 to replace an earlier Augustinian church on an adjoining site. The church is on the site of one of the first hospitals in Europe, built at the end of the twelfth century by Ailred the Dane and dedicated to St John the Baptist. The present building was designed by the eminent architects Edward Pugin and George Ashlin. Construction was halted several times due to lack of funds and was finally completed in 1895 when it was dedicated to St John the Baptist and St Augustine.

Among those who worked on the church was James Pearse, father of Padraig Pearse, a noted sculptor and stonemason of his day, who was responsible for the statues around the tower and for some work inside the church also. Of particular interest in the church is the shine to Our Lady of Good Counsel. There are also some striking stained glass windows. These include one by Michael Healy (outside the altar rails on the Good Counsel side) and two from the Harry Clarke Studios (on the opposite side) — which have recently been restored.

Opening hours
7.00 am - 8.15 pm daily

ST CATHERINE'S CHURCH, THOMAS STREET

St Catherine's Church was completed in 1769 and its north front, facing Thomas Street, is considered the finest classical church facade in Dublin. It was designed by the architect John Smith, who was also responsible for the design of the Poolbeg lighthouse.

References to St Catherine's Parish can be found as far back as the thirteenth century where it is often mentioned in the Christ Church deeds. During this time St Catherine's acted as a chapel of ease for the Abbey of St Thomas.

The church is interesting for its oak panelled gallery and good plasterwork at the eastern end. In the vaults behind the church are the remains of the Dublin historian, Dr Whitelaw, as well as several of the Brabazon family, Earls of Meath.

St Catherine's was closed in 1967 and was deconsecrated. Its original box pews and the eighteenth century organ were removed. However, a voluntary trust took a lease on the building and restored the interior so that the church could be used for concerts, meetings and exhibitions. In 1975, the European Architectural Heritage Year, the facade was cleaned and missing stonework was replaced by Dublin Corporation.

CHURCH OF ST CATHERINE OF ALEXANDRIA, MEATH STREET

A shrine to St Catherine is said to have existed in or about Meath Street from Danish times. St Catherine's Church first appears as a chapel of ease to the Abbey of St Thomas, which gave its name to Thomas Street and was built in 1177. This was the original parish church and remained such up to Elizabethan times.

In 1562 Elizabeth appointed a Protestant rector named Pye to take over the church. For a long time afterwards ecclesiastical records are blank and the local Catholics had to rely on the ministrations of brave priests who risked their lives to serve them. We do know that around the middle of the seventeenth century the parish chapel was in Dirty Lane (at the top of the present Bridgefoot Street).

The present site was obtained in 1782 and an octagonal church built there. It was back a little from the road and a presbytery was built in front of it.

The church we see today was built in 1852, on the site of the old church and presbytery, by Canon Laphen PP. With the aid of a committee, headed by Sir James Power, £1,000 was collected from the rich, and the contributions of weekly pennies by the poor in the Liberties raised double that amount. The foundation stone was laid by Dr Cullen, Archbishop of Dublin, on 30 June 1852. A silver trowel commemorating this event can still be seen in the parochial house in Meath Street. The new church, dedicated to St Catherine of Alexandria, was opened by Dr Whelan, Bishop of Bombay, in the unavoidable absence of Dr Cullen, on 30 June 1858.

Opening hours
Open all day

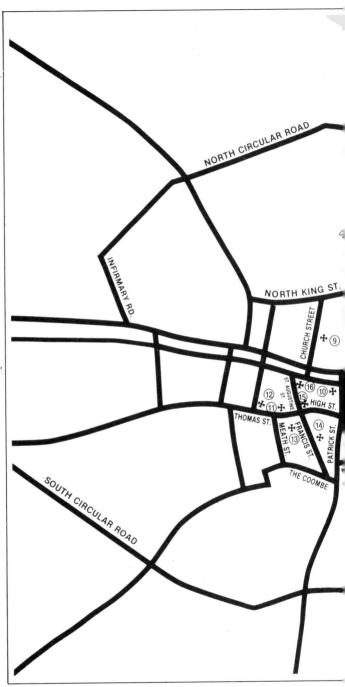

NORTH CIRCULAR ROAD

INFIRMARY RD.

NORTH KING ST.

CHURCH STREET

✝ ⑨

✝ ⑯ ⑩ ✝
ST. AUGUSTINE ST.
⑫ ⑮
✝ ✝ HIGH ST.
⑪ ✝

THOMAS ST.
✝
FRANCIS ST.
MEATH ST.
⑬ ✝ ⑭
PATRICK ST.

THE COOMBE

SOUTH CIRCULAR ROAD

34

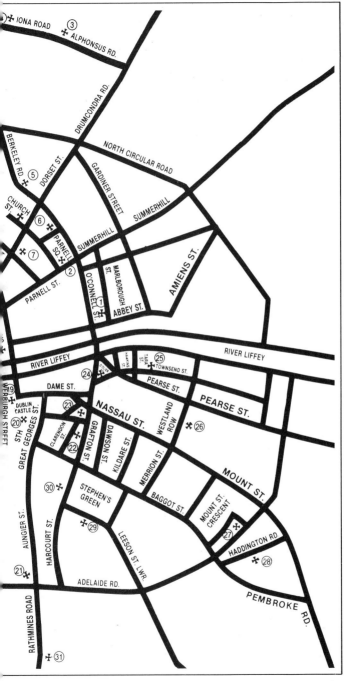

IONA ROAD
③ ALPHONSUS RD.
DRUMCONDRA RD.
NORTH CIRCULAR ROAD
BERKELEY RD.
⑤ DORSET ST.
GARDINER STREET
SUMMERHILL
SUMMERHILL
CHURCH ST.
⑥
PARNELL SQ.
SUMMERHILL
AMIENS ST.
⑦
② PARNELL ST.
MARLBOROUGH ST.
O'CONNELL ST.
① ABBEY ST.
RIVER LIFFEY
RIVER LIFFEY
⑲
DAME ST.
㉔
HAWKINS ST.
TARA ST.
㉕ TOWNSEND ST.
WERBURGH STREET
DUBLIN CASTLE ST.
㉓
NASSAU ST.
PEARSE ST.
PEARSE ST.
WESTLAND ROW
⑳ STH. GREAT GEORGES ST.
CLARENDON ST.
GRAFTON ST.
DAWSON ST.
KILDARE ST.
MERRION ST.
㉖
㉒
MOUNT ST.
⑳ ㉚
STEPHEN'S GREEN
BAGGOT ST.
MOUNT ST. CRESCENT
㉗
AUNGIER ST.
HARCOURT ST.
㉙
LEESON ST. LWR.
HADDINGTON RD.
㉘
㉑
ADELAIDE RD.
RATHMINES ROAD
PEMBROKE RD.
㉛

35

CHURCH OF ST NICHOLAS OF MYRA, FRANCIS STREET

The Church of St Nicholas of Myra is on the site of the original Franciscan church built in 1235. There have been several rebuildings since then, culminating in the building of the present church. Under the inspiring guidance of Archdeacon Matthew Flanagan, this majestic church took five painstaking years to build (1829-1834).

The pediment of the church is surmounted by statues of Our Blessed Lady, St Patrick and St Nicholas of Myra. On entering the body of the church, one's eyes are immediately drawn to the altar and the decorated ceiling. The altar was built in Italy and above and behind it is painted the symbol of an eye representing the all-seeing and all-providing God. Underneath this is a representation of the Holy Spirit in the form of a dove. Below this again is the beautiful Pièta, the work of the famous Irish sculptor, John Hogan. The apostles are painted on the ceiling above the sanctuary. Also on the ceiling are paintings of four early fathers of the church — St Gregory the Great, St Jerome, St Ambrose and St Augustine.

Two commemorative designs are also very prominent on the ceiling. One of these recalls the foundation of the Legion of Mary in the parish in 1921 while the other recalls the amazing fact that the Isle of Man once formed part of the parish of St Nicholas of Myra.

Opening hours
Open all day

ST AUDOEN'S CHURCH, CORNMARKET

The present church, dedicated to St Audoen, is of Norman foundation (c. 1190) with the addition of a chancel (c. 1300), the Guild Chapel of St Anne (1431) and the Portlester Chapel (1455). The oldest part of the present church is the nave and is the only part of the original building which is still roofed and used every Sunday for the Eucharist (Church of Ireland). St Audoen's is the only parish church of the city which retains its medieval ground plan and a large part of its medieval fabric intact. It was in the heart of medieval Dublin and was the church of the Lord Mayor and Corporation. The 'Three Castles' coat of arms of the city can be seen in the top light of the east window, one of two remaining fragments of early stained glass. A number of gravestones in the church mark the burial places of Lord Mayors and Aldermen of the city. In the sixteenth century St Audoen's Parish 'was accounted the best in Dublin for the greater number of Alderman and Worships of the city living in the parish'.

There is some inconclusive evidence that a church, dedicated to St Columba, existed on the site prior to the building of the present church. The evidence is in the form of 'the Lucky Stone', which can be seen in the porch leading from the tower to the church. It is an early Christian gravestone, or marker, probably dating from the eighth century, inscribed with a Celtic cross on both sides. It has a long association with St Audoen's, the earliest in 1309, when John Le Decer, the first Lord Mayor, set it up in Cornmarket beside the water trough. The stone may be original to the site or may have been brought as building material for the Norman church from the early Christian site at what is now St Patrick's Cathedral. Over the centuries the stone has disappeared from the church only to reappear in mysterious circumstances. In the 1860s the stone was set up in its present position, firmly fixed to the wall in case of any further disappearances! It is said that a ghost of a clergyman still stalks the passageway to St Audoen's Arch to protect the stone from would-be thieves!

Opening hours
Sunday 10.45 am   Communion service.

ST AUDOEN'S CHURCH, HIGH STREET

On Easter Monday 1841, the parishioners of St Audoen's met with their parish priest to plan the building of a new church. The serving parish chapel in Bridge Street had run its course. A site had been purchased for £4,436 from the proceeds of the famous weekly Penny collections. Daniel O'Connell, the Liberator, was present at this meeting. (The bell of the new church was afterwards to herald his release from the Bridewell and later to toll for his funeral.)

The new St Audoen's was blessed and opened on 13 September 1846 by Archbishop Murray. The sermon was preached by Dr Miley. The church had cost £4,483 to build and the architect was the famous Patrick Byrne (1783-1864).

The Great Famine delayed the interior decoration which was not completed until after 1860. The imposing facade was added in 1899.

The very fine high altar is clearly visible from all parts of the church. To the right, stands the award winning (1849) Carrara marble statue of Our Lady holding her Infant. It was specially executed in Rome by Peter Bonanni — much admired by Hogan. Another feature of the church is the wooden Walker Organ (1861). It has three manuals, forty-two stops and 2,300 pipes and is in excellent playing order.

The National Shrine to St Anne is marked by a Deghini-cast statue (Fishamble Street). Devotion to St Anne has been associated with St Audoen's since Norman times.

The holy water fonts at the church door are giant turtle shells from the South Seas — the gifts of a sea captain to his brother, a priest who served at St Audoen's.

The church ceased to act as a parish church in 1974 and is now the centre of the St Audoen Heritage Foundation (established 1987).

Opening hours

Daily	10.00 am - 5.30 pm
Closed for lunch	1.00 pm - 2.00 pm

41

CHRIST CHURCH CATHEDRAL

The Dean and Chapter of Christ Church welcome visitors to this historic cathedral, which is the mother church of the Diocese of Dublin and Glendalough in the Church of Ireland.

The Cathedral was founded in the year 1038 by Sitric, King of the Dublin Norsemen, for Dunan, first Bishop of Dublin, who erected a simple wooden church. After the coming of the Normans to Ireland in 1169 the church was rebuilt in stone by Richard de Clare, Earl of Pembroke (known as 'Strongbow') for St Laurence O'Toole, Archbishop of Dublin, who died in the year 1180 at Eu in Normandy. Visitors may see the monument to Strongbow in the south side aisle (on the right when facing the high altar) and the heart of St Laurence in the chapel of St Laud on the right of the Lady Chapel behind the high altar.

Leaflets and booklets are available to help you to discover for yourself the story and the glory of Christ Church Cathedral.

A cathedral is a place for solitary moments, a place one may go for peace and shade and rest, but it is also a place of great assemblies. Here in Christ Church, in the hallowed silence and the timelessness, many have found inward harmony and renewal of the springs of life.

As you go forth into the world again, we extend to you the eucharistic greeting:

'The peace of the Lord be always with you'.

Opening hours

May-September	10.00 am - 5.00 pm Monday to Saturday
	Between services on Sundays
October-April	Tues-Fri: 10.00 am - 4.30 pm
	Sat: 10.00 am - 1.00 pm
	Closed Mondays

ST PATRICK'S CATHEDRAL

St Patrick's Cathedral stands on the oldest Christian site in Dublin where it is said the Saint baptised converts to the Christian faith in a well beside the building. Beause of this sacred association with St Patrick a church has stood here since 450 AD. In 1191 that old church was replaced by the present building, the largest church in Ireland, which, as well as being a Cathedral, later became the first University of Ireland (1350-1520).

The famous Jonathan Swift who was Dean of St Patrick's (1713-1745) is buried in the Cathedral beside Stella. Here are also to be found old Celtic grave stones, medieval brasses and tiles, the medieval Chapter House door with a hole in it, dating from 1492 which gave the phrase 'chancing your arm' to the English language. The Earl of Kildare cut the hole and stretched out his arm to grasp the hand of his enemy, the Earl of Ormonde, who had taken refuge in the Chapter House. By taking the initiative reconciliation was achieved. In the choir are the banners and stalls of the Knights of St Patrick (1783) and in the transepts the old Irish regimental banners and monuments. Memorials to famous Irishmen abound in the Cathedral, including Carolan, last of the Irish Bards, Philpot Curran, Balfe the composer and Douglas Hyde, first President of Ireland.

The Choir School, founded in 1432, educates boys for the Choir who, together with the Lay Vicars Choral, sing two liturgical offices every day in the Cathedral.

The massive West Tower which houses the Cathedral bells, the largest ringing peal in Ireland, was built by Archbishop Minot in 1370 and the first public clock in Dublin was placed here in 1560.

Opening hours

Weekdays	8.30 am - 6.15 pm
Saturdays & Sundays	8.30 am - 5.00 pm

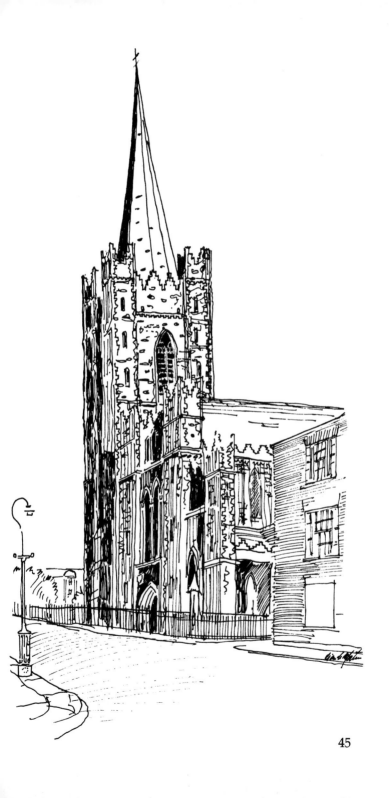

ST WERBURGH'S CHURCH, WERBURGH STREET

One of the oldest churches in Dublin, St Werburgh's can be found in Werburgh Street, off Christ Church Place. It is dedicated to St Werburgh, the patroness of Chester and was built during the reign of Henry II by the 'men of Bristol' who colonised the city.

St Werburgh's was, for a long time, the parish church of Dublin and was considered the most fashionable chapel in the city. Before the erection of the Chapel Royal in the Lower Castle Yard viceroys were sworn into office here.

Beneath the church can be found twenty-seven vaults, two of which are under the chancel. The remains of Lord Edward Fitzgerald are to be found enclosed in a coffin over seven feet long. Ironically, in the graveyard of St Werburgh's are the remains of Major Sirr who was instrumental in the capture and death of Lord Fitzgerald.

The Geraldine Monument, which once belonged to the Priory of All Hallows, can also be seen in St Werburgh's Church. The Geraldine Arms portray the recumbent figures of a knight in armour and his wife.

The church is renowned for a number of other facts. Handel played the organ there during his stay in Dublin while the celebrated James Usher, later the Archbishop of Armagh and Primate of Ireland, was appointed to St Werburgh's in 1607.

The tower and spire were added in 1768 but were taken down in 1810 and in 1836, the spire being removed first because the government disliked any structure having a possible field of fire into the Castle yard.

Opening hours
Sunday   8.00 am & 10.30 am Service

THE CHURCH OF THE MOST HOLY TRINITY, DUBLIN CASTLE

The Church of the Most Holy Trinity was once known as the 'Chapel Royal' and was the chapel of the viceroys. It was designed by Francis Johnston in 1807 and is known as one of his most famous works. The stucco work and the architectural ornaments are the work of Stapleton while the Smyth brothers were responsible for the sculpture and Stewart executed the oak carvings.

The viceroy's throne was situated on the south gallery. Oak panels over the aisles and on the chancel walls and the stained glass in the gallery windows depict the arms of all the viceroys from Baron Hugh De Lacey in 1173. An old legend claimed that once the last available space was used to portray a viceroy it would mark the end of an era. Ironically the arms of the last two viceroys can be seen in the last free places in the windows.

In 1813, Lord Whitworth presented the centre panels of the east window which depict scenes from the Passion of Christ. These were purchased by Lord Whitworth when he was ambassador to Paris in 1802. The exterior decorations include some eighty-six carved heads of English monarchs, oddly mixed with Our Lady, Dean Swift, St Peter and Brian Boru.

In 1943, the Chapel Royal became a Catholic Garrison Church and, on Whit Sunday of that year, was blessed by the Archbishop of Dublin.

Opening hours
Temporarily closed for repairs.

THE CHURCH OF OUR LADY OF MOUNT CARMEL, WHITEFRIAR STREET

The present church stands on the original site acquired by the Carmelites around 1280 and confiscated in 1539. In 1825 Fr John Spratt commenced the building of the new church, and the foundation stone was laid by Archbishop Murray of Dublin. The architect was Sir George Papworth who is believed to have designed the Pro-Cathedral the previous year. The church originally measured 200 feet by 34 feet and cost £4,000.

It was altered in 1842. The original building became the south aisle, a nave was added with an aisle on the north side, thus trebling the width of the original building. In 1852 it was decided to open an entrance from Aungier Street.

Over thirty years ago the church was overhauled and reversed. The main altar was changed from the Aungier Street end to the Whitefriar Street end and the Whitefriar Street entrance was closed. A new sacristy and shrine to St Thérèse of Lisieux was added.

The well-known Dublin historian and author, Eamon MacThomais wrote in the *Irish Press* (25 August 1986):

> . . . Anyone who has not been in this Church for some time would be well advised to make a visit soon. It has a brand new entrance hallway telling the story of the Carmelites in words and pictures.
>
> This Church has something for everyone, St Jude for the hopeless cases, St Valentine for the romantic cases, and the statue of the pregnant Our Lady for expectant mothers. . . .

Opening hours
7.30 am - 7.00 pm daily

51

ST TERESA'S CHURCH, CLARENDON STREET

St Teresa's dates from around the late 1780s. Until this time the Discalced Carmelites were at Wormwoodgate (Bridge Street) and then in Lower Stephen's Street (Dawson Court). In May 1786 the lease in their premises was up and the Carmelites were forced to look elsewhere. A committee of interested businessmen was set up to help in the search for a new site and in late 1786 an area behind some houses on Clarendon Street was found. Because of legal difficulties the order was not immediately able to start building.

On the 3 October 1793 the foundation stone was laid. The building took four years because of lack of funds. It was designed by the architect and builder, Timothy Beahan, in a rectangular style with the corners canted off. It was a three tiered building with extensive burial vaults beneath the chapel, the chapel itself and living quarters on the top of the chapel.

The church was finally finished in April 1797 and opened in May of that year.

The interior included a high altar at the south end with galleries on three sides and ninety family pews. The entrance was through the north side, where Switzers is today. In 1829 the Irish sculptor, John Hogan, returned from Rome with a newly-finished masterpiece, 'The Dead Christ'. It was exhibited at the Royal Irish Institution, College Street, where two friars bought it for £400. Hogan supervised its placing under the high altar, where it remains to this day. In 1865, the transept towards Grafton Street was built adding the transept, belfry and ornamental gateway which can be seen today. 1876 saw the building of the transept towards Clarendon Street and finally, the priory was built on the site of two houses which formerly belonged to Switzer's.

During the 1800s Daniel O'Connell was friendly with the friars and many political meetings concerning Catholic Emancipation were held in the years 1813 to 1829.

Opening hours
Open all day

53

ST ANDREW'S CHURCH, ST ANDREW'S ST

St Andrew's Church, sometimes referred to as the 'Round Church', is situated in the vicinity of St Andrew's Street and Suffolk Street. The church we see today has been in existence since the late eighteenth century. The old church of St Andrew's was totally demolished some years before the Restoration of Charles II.

In April 1670 it was decided that a new church would be built on the 'old bowling green' which was donated by Henry James, Bishop of Meath. The church was to be built in an oval shape based on a design by William Dodson, hence the name the 'Round Church'.

In 1745 the parish claimed the church was in a 'ruinous condition' and needed a new roof. John Hartwell was commissioned to plan the work in 1793.

In 1800 Hartwell resigned from his position and the work was eventually completed by Francis Johnston. The interior of the church was designed by James Lever. The Lord Lieutenant presented a large gilt chandelier to the parish which had once belonged to the Irish House of Commons and was later transferred to the Examination Hall in Trinity College.

During the years 1793 to 1807 the parishioners of St Andrew's had to be accommodated by the chapel in Eustace Street. Eventually on Sunday 8 March 1807, the church reopened, having cost in the region of £22,000 for its reconstruction.

Opening hours
10.00 am - 4.00 pm
Closed Monday

BLESSED SACRAMENT CHAPEL, D'OLIER STREET

The five outside pillars are topped by animal figures (e.g. turtle, hares, lobster . . .) indicating that this building was formerly the Red Bank Restaurant, since 1900. As James Joyce's funeral cortege passed by in 1941, it acknowledged his former presence therein.

The stained glass window indicates that it is now the Blessed Sacrament Chapel, blessed by Archbishop Charles McQuaid on 6 January 1970. The window itself is more recent (1985); it depicts the Holy Spirit transforming the bread and wine into the Body and Blood of Christ and thus extending the rays of life by those sharing Christ's life.

The chapel is directed by the Congregation of the Blessed Sacrament. The statue of its founder, Saint Peter Julian Eymard (1811-1868), is next to the window. He was canonised by Pope John XXIII in 1962.

The sanctuary-altar is in the middle between the D'Olier Street and the Hawkins Street sides of the chapel. The white stucco walls, as well as the low ceiling, create an atmosphere of the catacombs. The restructuring was designed by Robinson, Keefe and Devane.

A special feature of this chapel is to extend the value of the Mass by having all-day Exposition of the Blessed Sacrament. The permanent sacramental Presence of Christ is placed in a distinctive monstrance on the altar. This monstrance was designed by the Irish artist Enda King, and it was made by Alwright and Marshall, silversmiths of Fade Street.

Opening hours

Weekdays	7.00 am - 10.00 pm
Sundays	9.00 am - 10.00 pm
Bank holidays	8.00 am - 10.00 pm

PENAL DAY CHAPEL, TOWNSEND STREET

The Penal Day Chapel in Townsend Street existed from approximately 1750-1834 and had a chequered history. It was originally set up in a stable 'behind Lord Ely's house in Hawkin's Street' in 1731 to do duty for St Andrew's Parish.

A number of accidents resulted in plans to move the chapel elsewhere. In 1738 records refer to a panic which ensued after the roof collapsed, and in 1750 a chimney collapsed killing several people. Because of these accidents the chapel eventually moved to an old schoolhouse in Townsend Street and remained there until 1834 when St Andrew's of Westland Row replaced it.

Today, only the remains of the chapel can be seen and a plaque on the wall commemorates the fact that Father Matthew was ordained there by Archbishop Murray.

ST ANDREW'S, WESTLAND ROW

St Andrew's Church, Westland Row was built between 1831 and 1834. It was the first church to be built in the inner city on a main thoroughfare following Catholic Emancipation in 1829.

Early in the previous century (1713-1750) Catholics used as their parish church an old stable at the back of Lord Ely's house in Hawkin's Street — the site of the old Theatre Royal. A record of January 1750 tells us that 'a great storm blew down a tall chimney stack while Mass was going on, which, breaking through the roof of the old stable killed several of the congregation and wounded many'. This catastrophe necessitated the building of a 'hastily erected and badly constructed church' in Townsend Street, which served the needs of the parish from 1750 to 1833.

Following Catholic Emancipation Archbishop Daniel Murray decided to build a new church and suggested a site on Westland Row. This was met with some opposition but Daniel O'Connell, who was Chairman of the Parish Building Committee, persuaded everyone at a meeting called to discuss the issue with an eloquent speech which concluded:

> Too long have we Catholics been slaves and cowards; let us come forth into the light . . . we are no longer felons . . . leave Townsend Street . . . let us build our church in Westland Row.

The architect of the new church in Westland Row was James Bolger and the style is neo-classical. Work began in April 1832 and St Andrew's was blessed and opened for worship in January 1834. However the church was not finally completed until January 1841 when it was solemnly consecrated by Archbishop Murray.

Opening hours
8.30 am - 8.00 pm daily

ST STEPHEN'S CHURCH, MOUNT ST CRESCENT

St Stephen's Church, otherwise known as the 'Pepper Canister' or 'Pepperpot' church, is a very familiar Dublin landmark. It was opened and consecrated by the Archbishop of Dublin, the most Rev. William Magee, DD on Sunday 5 December 1824. The first chaplain was the Rev. W. Bourne, also chaplain of St Andrew's at that time.

The church was designed by John Bowden who was also the architect to the Board of Education and was known for his designs of courthouses. After Bowden's death the church was completed by Joseph Welland at a cost of £5,169. The site was owned originally by the Pembroke Estate who donated it and also contributed the sum of £100 towards the erection of St Stephen's.

The portico of the church is of the Ionic order while a belfry tower, octagonal in shape, can be seen rising over the pediment. The tower and dome are copies of Athenian models and rise to 100 feet.

The interior is an example of Victorian Renaissance, with spacious galleries and a flat, timber ceiling. The original box pews are no longer in the church. In 1852, extension work was carried out, adding the apse and the vestry. In the apse are three windows which depict various religious scenes. The centre window shows the stoning of St Stephen the martyr, while on the left we see Simon and Andrew leaving to join Jesus and, finally, on the right hand side, is the scene of Jesus with Mary and Martha. Similar scenes are depicted in other windows throughout the church. The pulpit dominates St Stephen's. It is canopied and carved in Italian rosewood. Four panels depict the symbols of the four evangelists.

Opening hours

Sunday	8.00 am	Holy Communion
	11.00 am	Matins and Address
	12 noon	Holy Communion
	6.30 pm	Evensong and Address
Wednesday	12.45 pm	Holy Communion

ST MARY'S, HADDINGTON ROAD

St Mary's, Haddington Road is a fine gothic revival church, its square tower an important landmark in the area. The building of the church commenced to a simple T-shape plan in 1835 and was opened and blessed on 4 November 1839. The architect is not recorded. In the 1870s an apse to the design of Charles Geoghegan was built while a decade or so later the present Haddington Road frontage designed by J. C. O'Callaghan and tower by Walter Doolin were added, extending the original three-bay nave by a further two. Aisles, in the decorated gothic style, followed to complete the church as it exists today.

The church was built by Arthur McKenna and Sons, Thomas Street, in limestone, ashlar, granite quoins and sandstone carvings. The facade to Haddington Road is a splendid example of gothic architecture with its rose, tourelle, general window tracery and tympana over the entrance doors.

Internally, there is some excellent stained glass including Irish windows by A. E. Child, Beatrice Glenavy and the Earley Brothers. There is a beautiful Madonna and Child opus sectile, also by the Earleys. The wall arcading and side altars in onyx and marble should also be noted, together with the carved oak communion rail and pulpit. Metalwork entrances to the baptistry and the mortuary are also excellent as are the floor and wall mosaics.

Memorials include one in marble to Most Reverend N. Donnelly DD, Auxiliary Bishop of Dublin and noted historian, and one in bronze to those who gave their lives in the 1914-18 war.

Opening hours
8.00 am - 8.00 pm daily

51

OUR LADY, SEAT OF WISDOM

The parish church of Our Lady, Seat of Wisdom, better known as Newman's Catholic University Church, was built in 1856. Although the basic ideas for the building and decoration of the church came from Father (later Cardinal) John Henry Newman, it is to his friend and colleague, John Hungerford Pollen, that credit is due for the material expression of these ideas.

The unattractive red brick exterior, and the large gateway-like entrance, hardly prepare one for the very beautiful little church within. Newman's idea was to build a large barn, and to decorate it in the manner of a Roman basilica with Irish marble and copies of standard paintings. Like most of the older churches in Rome, the interior is Byzantine in character, with a mixture of the ornate Italian style. The high altar, comprising a series of panels of choice specimens of Irish marble, stands within an apse beautifully painted in the medieval manner by Pollen. The organ choir on the gospel side of the sanctuary, and the splendid pulpit on the opposite side, are constructed of Irish marble. Slabs of the same material encrust the lateral walls, alternating with delicate semi-circular mosaics, representing patron saints.

Today University Church is not merely a memorial to the great Cardinal's artistic genius and good taste but a busy city-centre church and the most popular venue in the country for weddings.

Opening hours

Sunday	8.45 am - 6.30 pm
Mon-Fri	7.45 am - 6.00 pm
Saturday	9.30 am - 7.45 pm

THE UNITARIAN CHURCH, STEPHEN'S GREEN

The congregation now worshipping in Stephen's Green can trace its descent back to the very first congregation of Protestant Dissenters in Dublin during the reign of Elizabeth I of England. Early records have been lost, but we do know that there was a meeting-house in Wood Street, opened for worship in 1673. By 1764 they had built a new meeting-house in Strand Street which did not, however, last very long; the congregation worshipped there for just over 100 years.

In the early years of the eighteenth century there was a growing opposition to creedal tests and, increasingly, liberal theological thought was to be found in many old Dissenting congregations. This movement had its effect on the people of Strand Street and certainly by 1843 the Strand Street congregation thought of itself as distinctively Unitarian. The 1843 communion plates are inscribed: 'The Unitarian Congregation Strand Street'.

In 1857 a site was purchased in Stephen's Green and a design for a new church put out to open competition, the contract for the construction of a church finally being awarded to Lanyon and Lynn of Belfast. It was opened for worship in 1863.

In line with the general architectural spirit of the times it is a 'church', rather than a 'meeting-house', as of old. It is, in fact, a reasonably good example of Victorian Gothic, but its most notable feature is certainly its wealth of stained glass — French, Flemish and English — and a notable example of one of the first pieces executed following the revival of the Irish stained glass industry after the turn of the century. This, the main window of the church, stands over the communion table. Its subject matter was inspired by the late Rev. E. Savell Hicks, minister of the church from 1910-62.

Opening hours
Daily service at 11.00 am

OUR IMMACULATE LADY OF REFUGE, RATHMINES

The area of Rathmines became a parish in 1823 when it was separated from the parish of St Nicholas Without. Canon William Stafford was appointed as the first parish priest. However, for about six years the parish had no chapel, and mass was held in the priest's house in Portobello Place or else in Milltown or Harold's Cross.

Finally, in 1830 a small church was built on a site purchased from the Earl of Meath. It was a Gothic style church and was opened by Archbishop Murray in August of that year.

By 1850, however, the parish had expanded to such a degree that it was decided a new, bigger church should be built on the same site. The architect, Patrick Byrne, was appointed to oversee the project. In 1854 the church, which was modelled on the 'Greek Cross' style, was named and was inaugurated by the Archbishop of Dublin, Dr Paul Cullen, in 1856.

Disaster struck in 1920 when fire destroyed the church. Some items from the altar were saved but much of the decorative work was destroyed. Rebuilding began immediately under the eye of the architect, R. H. Byrne at a cost of almost £55,000. By 4 July 1920 the church was ready to be reopened, with the famous copper dome completing the building.

Today the church of Our Immaculate Lady of Refuge is very popular, especially with the young people of 'flatland', as is evident from the crowds attending the 6.00 folk mass each Sunday evening.

Opening hours
7.00 am - 7.00 pm daily